Hailey's

Gift

LindaMinor

Hailey's Gift

21st Century Press is a publisher dedicated to publishing books with high family values. We believe the vision for 21st Century Press is to provide families and individuals with user-friendly materials that enrich daily life and experience.

It is our hope that this book will help you discover truths for your life and enable you to meet the needs of others. May you be richly blessed.

21st Century Press
2131 W. Republic Rd. PMB 211
Springfield, MO 65807
800-658-0284
www.21stcenturypress.com

ISBN: 978-0-9911004-9-1
Cover Design: Lee Fredrickson
Book Design: Lee Fredrickson

21stCENTURY
P   R   E   S   S
READING YOU LOUD AND CLEAR.

This book is dedicated to Markus Owens and to
the loving memory of my precious
great-granddaughter
Hailey Marie Owens.

Born: August 18, 2003
Died: February 18, 2014

Proceeds from Hailey's Gift will go directly to the cost of publishing and printing additional copies of this book and to the Markus Owens Education and Welfare Fund.

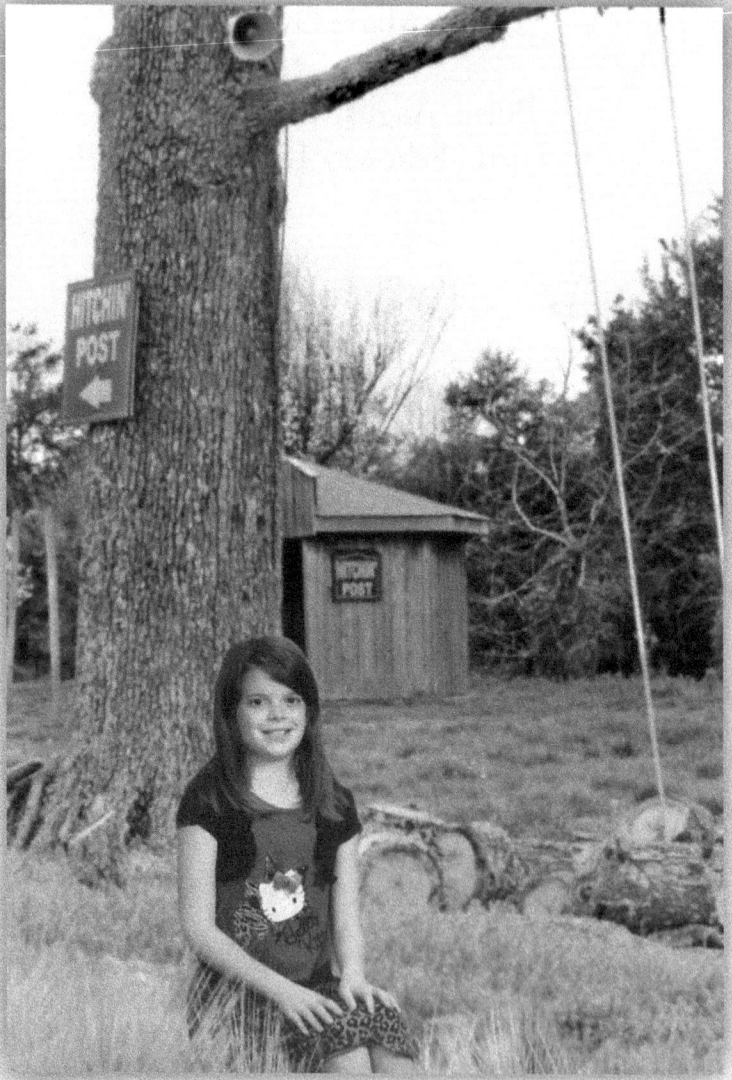

Acknowledgment

I would like to acknowledge and thank the people who helped me in bringing this book to completion.

First of all, to Rex Minor, my loving Christian husband, whom I cherish, for supporting me in every way possible in writing this book.

I also want to thank Andrea George, my good friend for spending countless hours taking my memories, thoughts and piles of notes, editing them and putting them onto the computer in book form.

To my daughter- in law, Tonya Minor for her suggestions and encouragements.

To her Great-Grandma Betty Herman for helping me collect pictures.

Linda Minor

Hailey's Gift

I am Hailey Marie Owens' great-grandmother. Hailey did not get to grow up and have a long life with us, but the time we spent with her will never be forgotten. I know she is in Heaven with Jesus. I know that one day I will get to be with Jesus and Hailey and spend eternity with them. It has not been easy for me to write this book because we miss Hailey very much. I believe Hailey would be pleased if her story could keep other children from being kidnapped or harmed.

My prayer is that parents will read this book to their children and will make it a daily resource to use in their lives. We need to start planting in the minds of our children, as young as two years old, how to be safe in this world. Our children and grandchildren are growing up in a cruel and evil world. It is our responsibility to equip them with safety rules and guidelines.

The purpose of this book is in no way suggesting how you should raise your children, for this is your responsibility and awesome pleasure. My goal is not only to remember Hailey Owens and her life, but to raise an awareness of the need for child safety and to bring it back as the number one priority in our homes and school.

Before you read this book, please take a moment to remember Hailey Maria Owens precious life. Hailey did nothing wrong on the day she was kidnapped and her life was taken. She was only doing what all little girls and boys like to do, Playing and having fun. It is Hailey's wish that all children be safer and smile their way through life.

Hailey was a precious little girl, full of life and joy.

Hailey's Story

Hailey Owens was a very pretty 10-year-old little girl who lived in Springfield, Missouri. She was in the fourth grade at Westport Elementary. She had many friends and classmates. She was always a happy girl and always made her classmates in school her friends. If her friends or classmates were sad or grumpy, she made them laugh with her big smile.

On February 18, 2014, in the afternoon, she walked to her friend's house to play. They had a great time that day. Hailey left her friend's house to return home for supper. She was walking alone on the sidewalk when a strange man in a pickup pulled up beside her and asked her for directions to a certain place. Hailey knew not to talk to strangers, so she kept on walking down the sidewalk towards her house. The strange man would not go away and pulled up beside her, opened the truck door, grabbed little Hailey, and drove off with her. She could not get away from him, even though she tried. He was a mean, evil man and he took her life. But her life didn't end that day, for you see, Hailey is enjoying eternal life in Heaven with her Heavenly Father and Jesus. This was a sad time for Hailey's family and friends, but it was also a time of joy, knowing that she was in a better place.

Hailey would want you to learn about being safe as you grow up, but more than that, she would want you to know where you will spend eternity. Following Hailey's story, in pictures, are a few things she would tell you so you can be safer as you grow up.

Jesus said, "Let the little children come to me, and do not hinder them, for the kingdom of heaven belongs to such as these." Matthew 19:14

Hailey had very pretty long brown hair. She liked getting it braided or put in a ponytail.

"'The Lord bless you and keep you; the Lord make his face shine on you and be gracious to you; the Lord turn his face toward you and give you peace." Numbers 6:24-26

Hailey liked playing with her Barbie dolls and stuffed animals. She placed all her stuffed animals on her bed.

"The wolf will live with the lamb, the leopard will lie down with the goat, the calf and the lion and the yearling together; and a little child will lead them." Isaiah 11:6

Hailey liked to play with little girls' makeup and got lots of jewelry for presents.

"Thanks be to God for his indescribable gift!"
2 Corinthians 9:15

Hailey's great-grandma Linda gave her a jewelry box filled with costume jewelry as a keepsake. She was very happy.

"Every good and perfect gift is from above, coming down from the Father of the heavenly lights, who does not change like shifting shadows." James 1:17

Hailey loved her mommy (Stacy) very much and spent a lot of time with her coloring pictures in her coloring books, helping her cook and clean house.

"And now these three remain: faith, hope and love. But the greatest of these is love." 1 Corinthians 13:13

Hailey liked getting her picture made with her mom, her brother Markus, her father Ryan, Aunt Erin, Aunt Chandra, her cousins, grandmas and great-grandmas.

"Look to the Lord and his strength; seek his face always."
Psalm 105:4

Hailey liked to dance with her mommy and her brother Markus. As she got older, she liked going to school parties and dancing with her friends.

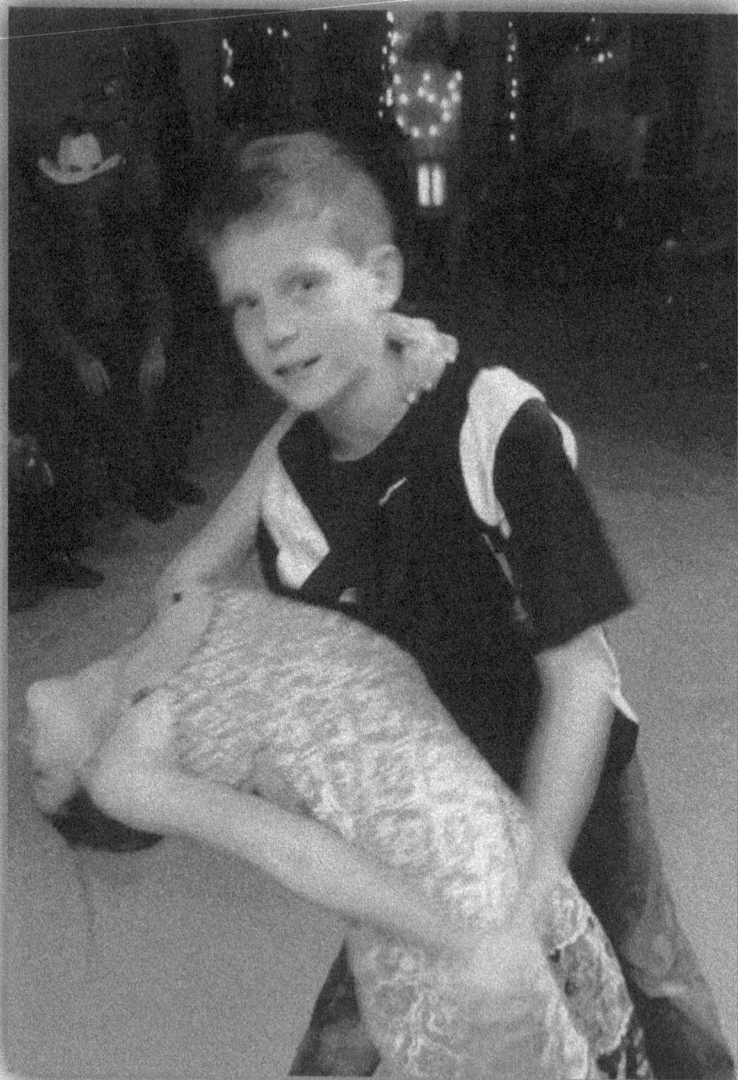

"Sing to Him a new song; play skillfully, and shout for joy."
Psalm 33:3

Hailey would walk with her mom and her brother Markus to the grocery store to buy food. She always stayed close to her mom while they were shopping.

"Honor your father and mother, and love your neighbor as yourself." Matthew 19:19

Hailey and her brother Markus were best of friends
and played together a lot outdoors because
she liked to climb trees.

"…there is a friend who sticks closer than a brother."
Proverbs 18:24

Hailey liked going to Hamlin Baptist Church
with her brother Markus.

"Worship the Lord with gladness; come before him with
joyful songs." Psalm 100:2

Hailey and Markus visited their great-grandma Betty and grandpa Roger in the summer. They live on a great big farm.

"Children are a heritage from the Lord, offspring a reward from Him." Psalm 127:3

Hailey and her brother got to ride on their grandpa Roger's tractor and wagon. Their grandpa would take them to the creek to look for "gold" rocks.

"They are more precious than gold, than much pure gold; they are sweeter than honey, than honey from the honeycomb." Psalm 19:10

Hailey went canoeing a lot with her mom, brother, and Grandpa Roger. Once they went canoeing for six miles down a river. That was a fun day for all of them. Camping was one of her favorite things to do.

"The sun has one kind of splendor, the moon another and the stars another; and star differs from star in splendor."
1 Corinthians 15:41

Hailey's cousins would come to visit their great-grandma and grandpa, too. Hailey and Markus had a great time playing with their cousins.

"See what great love the Father has lavished on us, that we should be called children of God! And that is what we are!" 1 John 3:1

Hailey also liked going with her brother to their great-grandma, Linda's house. Her great-grandma lives in the country with lots of trees and a big yard full of green grass where they would run and play. They had lots of fun picking wild flowers for a bouquet to give to great-grandma Linda to put in a vase of water.

"The Lord is my shepherd, I lack nothing. He makes me lie down in green pastures, he leads me beside quiet waters, he refreshes my soul. He guides me along the right paths for his name's sake." Psalm 23: 1-3

In the summertime, Hailey and Markus would spend time at their great-grandma Linda's house before going to the creek to go swimming.

"As the deer pants for streams of water, so my soul pants for you, my God." Psalm 42:1

After swimming for a while, they would stop back by great-grandma Linda's house. She would have milk and cookies and sometimes donuts for them to eat for swimming had made them hungry.

Then Jesus declared, "I am the bread of life. Whoever comes to me will never go hungry, and whoever believes in me will never be thirsty." John 6:35

Sometimes, Hailey would go shopping with her grandma Tammy and her aunt Chandra. They would buy Hailey new clothes. Her favorite colors were pink and purple.

"This is how we know that we love the children of God: by loving God and carrying out his commands." 1 John 5:2

Hailey always gave her great-grandma and grandpa a big
hug as she left to go home.

"We love because He first loved us." 1 John 4:19

Hailey enjoyed her school. She attended Westport Elementary School in Springfield, Missouri. She always made her friends smile, and she made new students feel welcome.

"Dear friends, since God so loved us, we also ought to love one another." 1 John 4:11

A playground at Westport School Park was recently dedicated in memory of Hailey. She would love for you to play in her playground. It is called Hailey's Playground.

"For God so loved the world that he gave his one and only
Son, that whoever believes in him shall not
perish but have eternal life."
John 3:16

Hailey's Safety Rules for Younger Children

1. Never walk alone, whether you are a boy or girl.

2. When walking on a sidewalk, always walk on the side closest to a yard or house - never,close to the street.

3. If you are approached by a stranger (male or female) in an automobile, never stop to talk to them. Run, run, run away from the stranger.

4. Never be afraid to scream for help. Remember, scream and run, scream and run, scream and run away!

5. Never go to a park without your mom and dad.

6. If you are playing in a park and someone tries to get you to go with them to look for a pet, never go. Run away from the stranger.

7. Don't ride your bicycle alone, because there are too many bad people who want to harm you.

8. If a stranger grabs you, scream, kick, and scratch him or her to get away. Then run to your house, school, or a trusted neighbor's house.

9. If you have ever been touched by someone in an inappropriate place on your body, never be afraid to tell your parents or teacher. You are not a bad person for telling.

10. Always remember what your parents and Hailey have taught you so that you can be safe in the world as you grow up.

11. Hailey wants you to learn to be safe.

Tweens...Be Aware

Tweens, I want to enrich in your minds how important it is to stay safe. It seems, as teens, your minds are filled with education, school activities, and church activities. What is going on around us is not always seen. Don't ever underestimate the evil that is in this generation. Don't get me wrong, there are a lot of good people, too. You need to be able to determine good from evil.

You are becoming closer to becoming an adult and gaining more independence from mom and dad than ever before in your life. Having your own car and going places by yourself calls for safe keeping. Remember what you have learned about being safe through the years. You will be around so many people at ballgames, concerts, parks, and numerous other places. Ever more so, you should be conscience of who is around you. Life is not easy as a teenager and being safe seems to be getting harder all the time.

The day of technology has filled your lives with so much information that your life can be consumed with watching television, working on computers, texting, and talking on cell phones. You might think you are safe in the community, but that might not be the case. Don't get me wrong, I am not against technology. I like my smart phone and use it daily. I want to stay connected to my friends and family as well. I am trying to stress that we should not be so consumed with technology that it causes us to be unaware to what is going on around us.

Hailey's Safety Rules for Tweens

1. Be aware of what is going on around you.

2. Watch for strangers hanging out near you.

3. Never be ashamed or afraid to report anyone who might be unsafe to be around.

4. Learn to be aware of classmates who are saying or displaying odd behaviors.

5. Be careful on the computer. Do not "friend" someone on the computer unless you know them in real life.

6. Do not share your personal information online.

7. When you are on your cell phone, iPads, or listening to music with headphones, be alert to what is going on around you.

8. Put to use the things Mom and Dad have taught you about being safe. Good common sense will help a lot.

9. We know our schools are not even safe anymore, so if you suspect anything strange, report it immediately.

10. Know your friends! Seek friends who have the same interests as you.

11. Remember Hailey Owens. Memorize her safety rules. She wants you to be safe.

Thoughts for Parents

I am Hailey's great-grandmother on her biological father's (Ryan Owens) side of the family, and I have raised three children of my own. I am over 70 years old, and I have seen a lot of changes in our society and world in my lifetime. My life and school days were spent in the country. We walked to a one-room schoolhouse on a main road and never did we feel unsafe. We rode our bikes, if fortunate enough to have one, all over the county where we lived to play with neighbor children. We walked by ourselves through the woods to our cousins' house to play, and the only thing we had to be afraid of was the farmer's bull in the field. But, times have changed. You may wonder if there is any place a child is safe nowadays. I would like to say yes, but I don't believe that is true anymore.

By the time my children started to school, there were no more country schools. Children had to ride school buses to school. If children lived close to school, they could walk on the sidewalks and be fairly safe. Now, I watch my grandchildren and great-grandchildren trying to grow up in a very evil world. Yes, times have changed a lot in the past 70 years. Parents, the day of trusting and taking for granted that your child is safe in this world is long gone.

Today, in this fast paced world we live in, our children have so many attractions to catch their attention. They are involved in many activities that put them more in jeopardy of being kidnapped by strangers around them. Our world is filled with so much technology, and children and parents can get so consumed with their devices. A good down to earth talk with your children about their safety is of the utmost importance. Spend more time with your children.

On behalf of Hailey Owens, I am encouraging all parents to teach their children about child safety. We live in a cruel and evil world, and it isn't getting any better. Child safety needs to be stressed more than ever before. It needs to be taught in the home and in school. I know child safety has been addressed in the past, but I'm afraid we have gotten slack in teaching our children about safety in this fast-paced world and society we live in. It is not our children's fault that so many people have become so cruel in this world. That is why I feel the need to stress child safety in this book in honor of Hailey's life.

I am in no way trying to tell you how to raise your children. I want to raise the awareness about child safety. Each child born into this world is a precious gift from God, and we must do all we can to protect them. Let's keep our children safe so no other child will be taken from us. No child should ever be kidnapped, hurt, or have their life cut short in a tragic way.

So, parents, let's start teaching child safety in the home more than we ever have. As your children grow into their school years, they will have embedded in their minds how important child safety is for them. Teach your children from year to year, as they grow up, about child safety, and by the time they are around 12 years old, it will be grounded into their minds. If we don't teach it to them when they are young, by the time they are about 12 years old, they are getting more away from mom and dad's apron strings. I'm not saying they are safe by themselves at that age, but they will certainly be more cautious of who is around them. The reason for drilling child safety at home, school, and any organization you might belong to is because by the time children reach the age of 12 years old they are already teetering between a child and a teen. Children seem to have much more freedom today at the age of 12 than when I was growing up.

Children are a precious creation and gift from God, and He never wants them to be hurt.

Hailey's Song

Jesus loves the little children,
All the children of the world,
Red and yellow, black and white,
They are precious in His sight,
Jesus loves the little children of the world.

Helpful Safety Rules to Share with Your Children

1. Start teaching child safety to your children as young as two years old.

2. Read child safety books to your children. They will remember more than you think, even if it's just a word or two.

3. Teach child safety at the dinner table, at bedtime, and everywhere you take your child.

4. Make your children aware, more than ever before, that they must be aware of who is around them, and to know if they are being followed.

5. Place a child safety sticker on your refrigerator reminding you to talk to your child about safety. It will also show your child it is something important to learn.

6. Know what your child is doing on the computer.

7. Know who your child is talking to on his or her cell phone or smartphone.

8. Keep your children by your side, even in a grocery store, department story, gas station, or anywhere you might be with them.

9. Tell your children you love them. Let them know you are always there for them.

10. If you do not have a church home, I encourage you to take your children to hear about God's love for each one of them.

11. Read Hailey's Safety Rules to your children.

Hailey's Most Important Gift

When Hailey was on earth, she wanted all boys and girls to know Jesus as their Saviour. Hailey is in Heaven with Jesus because she had asked Him to be her Savior and Lord of her life. She is very happy in Heaven playing with other children and drawing pictures in the sand.

Just like Hailey, it is my prayer that all men, women, girls, and boys will believe in Jesus Christ and accept Him as their Savior. If you would like to ask Jesus to be your personal Savior, please know it is simple as A-B-C.

Admit you're a sinner.

Believe in Jesus as your Savior.

Choose to follow Jesus.

Admit you are a sinner. Everyone sins. In Romans 3:23, it says, "For all have sinned and fall short of the glory of God."

Believe that Jesus died on the cross to forgive and remove your sins so you can really live as His child now and forever.

Choose to follow Jesus. Happiness that will last forever comes from knowing God's plan of salvation and following Him!

God loves you. In John 3:16, Jesus said, "For God so loved the world that he gave his one and only Son, that whoever believes in him shall not perish but have eternal life."

If you would like to receive Jesus as your personal Savior, pray the following prayer from your heart.

Dear Jesus,

I know that I am a sinner, and I ask for Your forgiveness. I believe You died for my sins and rose from the dead. I turn from my sins and invite You to come into my life. I want to trust and follow You as my Lord and Savior.

In Your Name I pray this prayer,

Amen

If you accepted Christ as your personal Saviour today, find a church where you can worship and serve Him.

Hailey's life has touched many hearts in this world. I pray that her life and story has touched yours.